I0757257

To Owen and Noah:

The chaos, the clarity, the candy economists.

You make everything worth it.

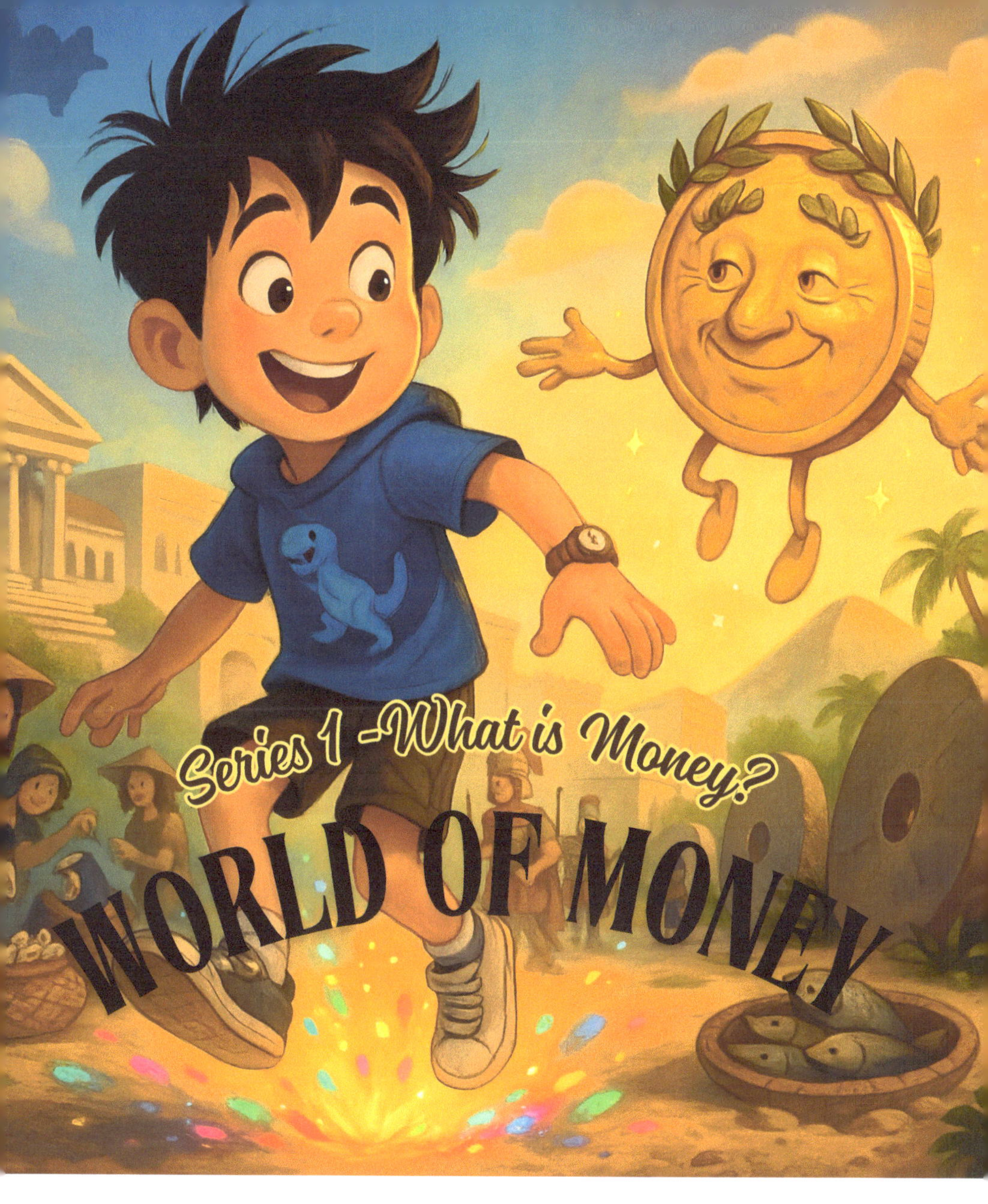

Written by Iris Wang
Illustrated by Iris Wang

with creative assistance from Nova
(a.k.a. Chat GPT-powered AI co-creator)

Copyright © 2025 Iris Wang
All rights reserved.

No part of this publication may be reproduced, stored in a retrieval system, or transmitted in any form or by any means—electronic, mechanical, photocopying, recording, or otherwise—without the prior written permission of the publisher, except in the case of brief quotations used in book reviews or scholarly articles.

First Edition
Printed in the United States of America

ISBN: [979-8-9995086-1-4]

Written by: Iris Wang
Illustrated by: Iris Wang, with creative assistance from Nova
(a.k.a. her ChatGPT powered AI co-creator)

Some illustrations and creative support in this book were generated in collaboration with ChatGPT, an AI developed by OpenAI, and lovingly guided by Iris Wang.

This book is a work of fiction inspired by historical facts and economic concepts. Names, characters, and events are used creatively for educational purposes.

For more information and materials in the *World of Money* series, visit: [www.theworldofmoney.com]

In a creaky old attic that smelled like cinnamon dust and secrets,

a boy named Noah rummaged through his grandpa's treasure chest.

Chapter 1

The Shiny Discovery

CLINK! CLANK! CLUNK!

In a creaky old attic that smelled like cinnamon dust and secrets, a boy named Noah rummaged through his grandpa's treasure chest.

Not the toy kind.

A real one — solid oak, brass hinges, ancient as bedtime itself.

Noah's fingers brushed something cold and round.

Aha!

He yanked it out—and gasped.

A golden coin lay in his palm, glowing warm like a pocket-sized sun.

Symbols shimmered across its surface, flickering like ancient fireworks caught mid-sparkle.

One side of it gleamed with the fierce face of a lion.

The other… blinked.

"*Wha—?*" Noah leaned in.

Suddenly,

"Well, hello there!"

A cheerful but slightly raspy voice came from the coin.

Noah yelped and nearly tossed it across the attic.

"D-Did you just… *TALK*?"

The coin smiled.

Literally, *smiled.*

A tiny mouth curled beneath two twinkling eyes.

It did a smooth backflip, like it had springs for edges.

"Name's Midas," The coin declared.

"Time-traveling, wisdom-giving, sparkle-filling companion."

"And you, my curious friend, are about to enter…

"the **World of Money**!"

Noah blinked.

"The world of *what* now?"

"*Money*!" Midas said, striking a superhero pose.

"You know, that mysterious stuff grown-ups are always chasing.

"But it's not what you think." The coin winked.

"It's not just the jingles in your piggy bank or the crisp bills in your mom's purse." Noah squinted.

"Wait, are you some kind of magical bank account?"

"*Pfft*. Please." Midas snorted.

"I'm *WAY* cooler."

Just then—

WHOOSH!

Golden light exploded through the attic.

The wooden floor softened beneath Noah's feet like honey melting off toast.

"*WhaaaAAAH!*"

He hollered, arms flailing as the world spun like a snow globe in a toddler's hands. He clutched Midas tight.

Shapes and colors whirled past:

stampeding buffalo, bustling markets, flashing neon signs.

He saw traders shouting, ships sailing, robots blinking, and kids his age handing over shiny rocks for… honey combs?

The coin smiled.

Literally, smiled.

His heart thudded like a snare drum.

Noah loved money.

He had counted his allowance twice this morning just to hear the clink.

He had once tried to open a candy store using Monopoly cash, sadly it didn't go well.

But this?

This was something else.

"Where are we going?"

Noah shouted over the roar of swirling wind.

"To the very beginning," said Midas,

glowing like a firefly dipped in gold.

And then—

The world snapped into place.

Golden light exploded through the attic.

Chapter 2

Fishy Trades Fail

THUD!

Noah's feet sank into cool, damp earth. Animal hides rustled in the breeze.

He stood in a smoky cave, its walls painted with ochre handprints and charging bison.

The air smelled like campfire and wet fur.

"Whoa," Noah whispered, taking it all in.

Around a crackling fire, people in leather tunics gathered, arguing over a pile of fish and fuzzy cloaks.

"Two furs for this fat fish!"

A woman with braided hair and bear-tooth necklaces thrust a fish to a man standing next to her.

It looked like it was some trout, bigger than Noah's arm.

"I don't want fish, I want axes!" growled the man, holding a carved spear and a sleepy wolf cub.

Noah tilted his head,

"Why don't they just… trade?"

He whispered to Midas.

Midas hovered closer and lowered his voice too, so they didn't attract attention from this tense crowd:

"Ah, that's the problem with bartering. You need a double coincidence of wants…"

"A *what*-now?"

"It is a fancy way of saying both people have to want what the other has." Midas laughed,

"and by the look of it, those fishes are more alive than the deal!"

Noah giggled and nodded in agreement.

He spotted something lurking deeper in the cave, and tiptoed forward to explore.

A pile of rainbow-scaled fish just sat forgotten in the corner, their gills barely moving. One flopped off with a wet splat.

The stench made Noah's eyes water.

"Ugh!" Noah pinched his nose. "Did a skunk marry a garbage truck?!"

"See? Another problem!" Midas chuckled.

"Fish rot, furs get moth-eaten—

they need something that lasts. Something that holds value."

Noah snickered: "This system stinks!"

A barefoot kid, who looked about Noah's age, slipped past them clutching a honeycomb.

He offered it to another child in exchange for a smooth river stone.

Soon a whole swarm of kids buzzed around, trading colorful pebbles for sticky honey drips.

Noah watched and grinned.

"It's like when I traded my rare Charizard trading card for five common ones. Worst. Deal. Ever."

"Without a set value, trading felt like...guessing."

Before he could think a bit more,

ZING!

A streak of golden comet-light spiraled around Noah's legs. It zipped up his body like a warm hug from a very opinionated flashlight.

"Wait—is this light alive?"

He yelped, grabbing for Midas.

But before Midas can answer...

The smoky cave already melted into a shimmering haze.

ZING!
The light zipped up his body like a warm hug
from a very opinionated flashlight.

Chapter 3

The Great Money Makeover

WHOOSH!

A salty breeze smacked Noah in the face like a wet towel.

He stumbled onto a golden beach the shape of a crescent moon. Palm trees swayed overhead, and soft waves lapped at the shore.

"*Ahhh!*" Noah sighed, brushing sea mist off his eyebrows.

"Now this is more like it!"

Nearby, ancient Chinese women in indigo robes knelt in the sand, threading shiny cowrie shells onto strings like sparkly pasta necklaces.

Their hands moved fast, their laughter travelled faster.

"Ten shells for one pottery bowl!"

A merchant called, his bamboo hat flapping in the wind as he held up a clay dish.

"Wait, they're using *seashells* as money?" Noah blinked. "I thought they are not worth anything?"

"Only this kind of shells," said Midas, bobbing in the air. "Rare, look similar and easy to carry, and they don't rot!"

"These beauties checked all the boxes back then as money."

"Well now I know a bit more about trades, the bowl is worth 5 shells. Tops!" Noah snorted.

"But also...money used to be beach jewelry?"

Noah stared at the shells, still struggling to believe it.

How could something you find just lying in the sand, be worth anything at all?

"You can say that.

"Money isn't always about what it is—it's about what people *agree* it's worth."

"Ten shells for one pottery bowl!"

Midas's eyes twinkled as he leaned closer.

"And kiddo, you haven't seen the least of the strange money… *yet*!"

Suddenly—

CRACK!

Thunder rolled as they appeared in ancient Rome.

Rows of soldiers in polished bronze armor marched past, their sandals squelching in the mud.

One soldier's pouch jostled open, spilling tiny white crystals onto the cobblestones.

Noah scooped a pinch.

"*Salt*? They were paid in salt?"

"Yup! Not just for flavor, either."

Midas hovered over the spilled crystals like a professor with sprinkles.

"The word *salary* actually comes from **Sal**, Latin for salt," he explained.

"Back then, salt was rare, precious, even life-saving. Roman soldiers were sometimes paid with it."

As if thinking of something, Midas smiled.

"And that's why sometimes your mom says you're 'worth your salt'!"

Noah shook his head,

"I'd take seashells over salt any day!"

"That's why sometimes your mom says you're 'worth your salt'!"

Then—

BOOM!

Next thing he knew, they stood in a jungle clearing on Yap Island under a blazing sun.

In the center, loomed a limestone wheel that was taller than Noah's house, with a hole in the middle big enough to hula-hoop through.

Villagers in grass skirts gathered around it, pointing and chanting, "That's Chief Oolong's money!"

Noah's jaw dropped. "That? That's *MONEY*?"

He ran up and shoved the stone wheel with both hands. It didn't budge even an inch.

"How do you even spend it?" asked Noah.

"You don't," said Midas, chuckling. "It just sits there. Everyone remembers who it belongs to, so you don't need to move it."

"That's crazy!" Noah cried. "What if someone forgets?"

Midas thought about it for a second, "Well, then it's up to the whole village and the chief to decide the *truth*."

Noah ran his fingers over the sun-warmed stone.

It reminded him of the smooth skipping rocks he collected—how he had argued with his friends about which one was the best.

He scratched his head. "So… money doesn't have to look like money?"

"As long as everyone agrees it's valuable, it counts?"

"Exactly," Midas nodded. "Money is a *shared belief*."

Midas paused, his eyes flickering dimly for a second.

"But belief can sometimes lead us… too far."

"That's Chief Oolong's money!"

Midas turned back to Noah, voice steady again.

"Whether it's shells, salt, or giant stone wheels the size of minivans, it all comes down to what people *trust*."

He pointed toward the bustling crowd, then to Noah's chest.

"Money's really just a **symbol**—a shortcut we all agree on."

"A way to measure value, trade things, and keep score. But it only works… if we *believe* it does."

Noah's eyes lit up, and a grin spread across his face.

"Cool! So if I convinced my class that my sock drawer was 'Fort Knox', then —"

"Let's not spark an economic revolution, just yet,"

Midas cut in, his eyes twinkling with amusement.

Suddenly, the ground trembled like a soda can ready to explode.

Rainbow confetti-light burst beneath Noah's sneakers, hoisting him into the air like a naughty helium balloon.

"Whoa! Midas!"

He laughed, kicking at the shimmer.

"Do I need a seat belt for this?!"

"Too late!"

Midas called out as they spiraled far into the sky.

"Midas- do I need a seatbelt for this?!"

Chapter 4

The Gold That Roared

FLASH!

Noah blinked twice in a wave of dazzling gold light.

When his eyes adjusted, he found them standing in a grand courtyard under a cloudless blue sky.

Not far from them, shirtless men poured molten gold into clay molds like liquid sunshine. A furnace shaped like a roaring lion belched flames, its heat making the air shimmer.

The smell of hot metal and olive oil clung to Noah's clothes.

"Where are we?" Noah murmured, eyes wide.

"Ancient Lydia, in Turkey!" Midas gleamed.

Swirling in his palm like a feather caught in a breeze. "Home of the world's *first* stamped coins!"

Just then, "BEHOLD!" A voice boomed.

King Croesus strode forward, his gold cufflinks flashing.

"This is a gold coin, and it is the *future*!"

He announced proudly, "Now my soldiers can carry wealth in their pockets!"

The king tossed more coins into the air. The crowd beneath him cheered like wildfire.

Noah couldn't resist. He lunged, snatching a coin mid-air.

It was warm, heavier than he expected. The lion's etched mane gleamed on its face.

"Whoa," Noah gasped and lifted it closer to his eyes.

"So cool... wait—"

"This looks just like *YOU*, Midas!" He shoved it to the coin himself. "Here, you should see!"

Midas's smile faltered, just for a heartbeat.

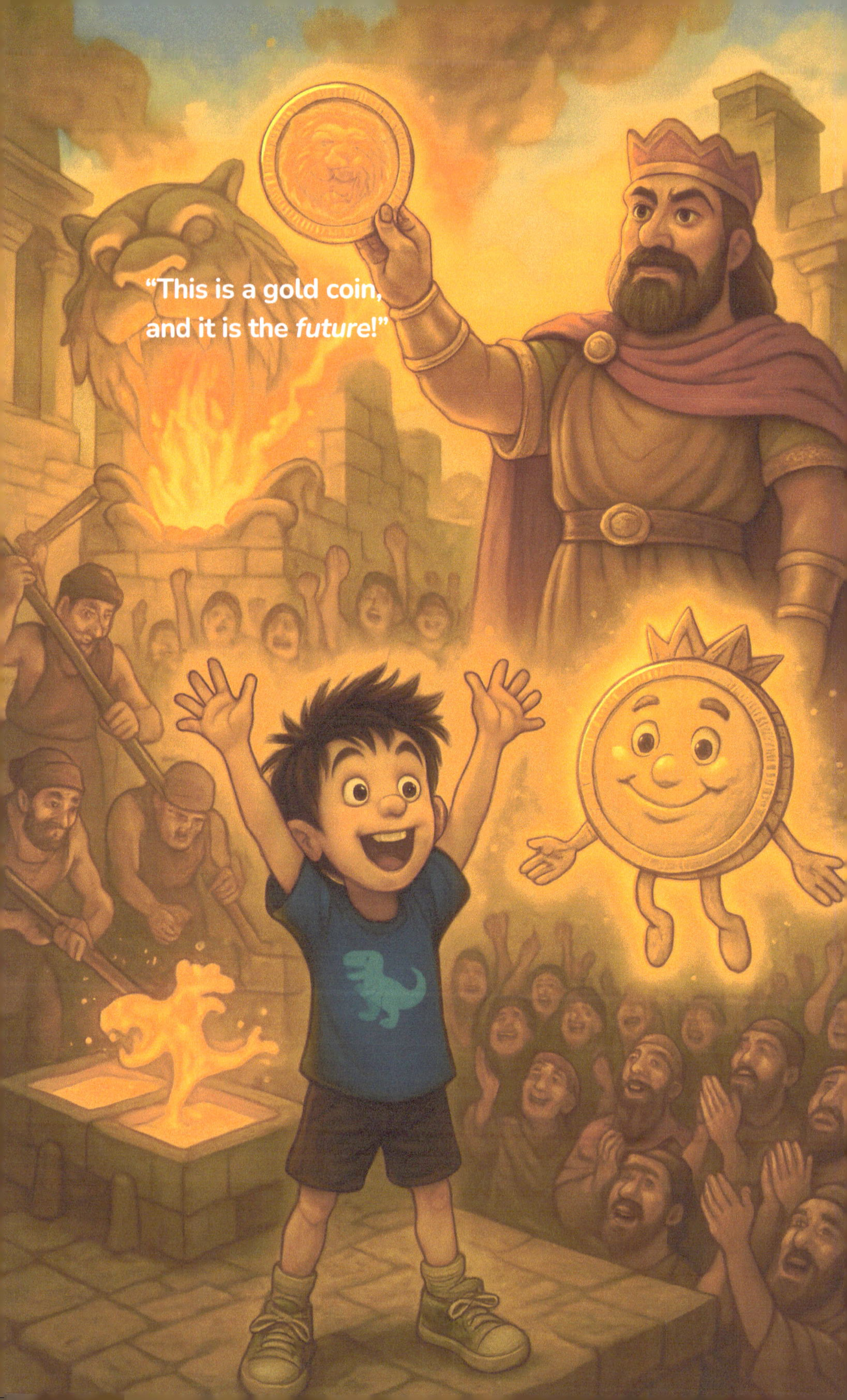
"This is a gold coin,
and it is the future!"

"Yes… perhaps too much like me."

He did not reach for it, but explained:

"Coins last a very long time, are made of rare gold, and can be split into smaller piece — perfect for trading."

Noah imagined buying pizzas with ancient coins.

"Way better than smelly fish and giant stone wheels!"

Around them, workers stacked coins into cedar wood chests.

The sound reminded Noah of his piggy bank at home—how satisfying it felt to drop coins in, watching his "fortune" grow.

Here, in this dusty courtyard where history was being made, Noah's shoulders squared.

His chest swelled, proud as the lion stamped on those very first coins.

He felt it right there: the weight of gold, and the desire to have it. Money isn't just stuff —

It's a real power you can hold, with your own hands.

Little did he notice, Midas's eyes were not as bright and cheerful as usual this time. There was the slightest flicker of sadness on his face.

And he was too distracted to hear Midas mutter under his breath, like a sigh:

"Gold's shiny… until it's all you see."

A breeze stirred, a stream of golden light started to pool around Noah's ankles, swirling faster and faster.

"C'mon, Midas—faster!"

He whooped, bouncing on his toes like a spring.

 The air hummed with possibilities:

What's waiting next?

Money isn't just stuff —
it's a real power you can hold,
with your own hands.

The air hummed with possibilities:
What's waiting for them next?

Chapter 5

The Emperor's IOUs

SWISH!

The first thing Noah felt was a flurry of white flakes, which landed right inside of his nose.

"*Ah-CHOO!*" He sneezed, "Midas, what is this stuff?!"

Rubbing his nose, he squinted as the attic's shadows sharpened into a bustling workshop—like a dragon's art class gone wild.

Men in flowing indigo robes hurried past, arms stacked with damp paper sheets as wide as pizza boxes.

Ka-CHUNK! Ka-CHUNK!

Wooden blocks carved with coiling dragons slammed onto the pages, stamping them with crimson symbols that shimmered faintly—like ancient spells written in red ink… or maybe really fancy ketchup.

The air smelled of ink and mulberry, thick enough to taste.

Midas buzzed in Noah's palm, his voice a hushed squeak of awe.

"Welcome to the Song Dynasty in China, little one. Where paper money was born!"

Noah peeked over a stack of bills. "Wait—*this* is money? It's just… paper."

Noah gave it a poke. It crinkled in his fingers, and reminded him of his homework.

"Yes and No," Midas grinned.

"It's not about paper, it's about the trust behind it."

"People believed their emperor would swap these for real gold anytime. Like an IOU… but fancier." Midas explained.

Suddenly, a stern official in a black-feathered hat stomped past.

"Forgers shall be punished with… *death!*"

It's not about paper -
It's about the *trust* behind it.

He bellowed, slamming a marble seal so hard that the pheasant feathers on his hat trembled.

"Note to self," Noah gulped,

"No Monopoly money scams in ancient China."

He caught a glimpse of several monstrous iron chests along the walls.

Their surfaces rippled with engraved dragons, claws outstretched as if ready to soar off the metal—or maybe guard whatever treasure lay inside.

Then—

POOF!

The inky scent of China vanished, replaced by the musty tang of old books.

They stood in a cramped London shop in the 17th century, where goldsmiths in dusty white wigs hunched over desks, scratching quills like chickens digging for worms.

Noah's eyes locked onto the iron-barred vault behind them.

"Whoa." His eyes opened wide as he saw rows of gold bars gleamed inside, stacked like forbidden chocolate.

Beside them, a ledger book lay open on a pedestal.

Pages crammed with numbers that climbed higher than Noah's shadow.

"This paper," croaked an old goldsmith, waving a receipt to the crowd lining up,

"proves that your gold is safe in our King's vault!"

His ink-stained fingers shook as if the paper weighed a thousand pounds.

Midas hovered closer, tapping the yellowed receipts with a knowing grin.

"They didn't call them banknotes yet," he explained,

"but these receipts let ordinary people trade without lugging around sacks of heavy coins."

"They could buy anything — from a loaf of bread to a cargo ship — just by trusting this promise."

Noah's eyes widened. "So… it wasn't the paper itself that was valuable…

"But the *promise* behind it?"

"Exactly," Midas nodded.

"That trust turned these slips of paper into something as powerful as gold itself."

Noah thought about the IOUs he had scribbled on torn notebook pages at home. His brother Owen had stopped accepting them after Noah "forgot" to pay him back.

Heat crept up his neck.

"So…money *only* works if everyone keeps their word."

"Bingo," said Midas, floating a bit higher.

"The very first seeds of modern banking. A system built on faith — and on people believing in each other."

Noah stared at the inky paper fluttering in the old goldsmith's hands.

Somehow, it felt even more magical than the lion-stamped coins.

A treasure you couldn't see,

but could still carry with you.

"Maybe next time I would honor the notes to Owen when I play Monopoly."

Noah thought to himself, as the air around them cracked with electric lemon-yellow sparks.

Noah's hair stood on end.

"Is the light angry?" he chuckled.

Midas just smirked.

"Nope—it's impatient!"

Chapter 6

Money in the Matrix

BZZZZT!

Everything turned pixelated.

Noah floated in a digital cosmos, where dollar signs zipped past him like shooting stars, QR codes zigzagged like laser tag beams, and app icons somersaulted through the air.

His skin prickled with static, his eyes darted faster than a hummingbird's wings— everything moved at turbo-speed.

"Whoa!" Noah shouted, ducking as a giant emoji nearly smacked him in the face.

"Did we just get sucked into a video game?!"

"Nope! Welcome to the **Digital World of Money**!" A shimmering coin with sunglasses and hover boots appeared beside them.

Midas beamed.

"Noah, meet Goldie. She's our tour guide to invisible cash!"

She gave Midas a high-five, throwing off tiny sparkly fireworks.

"The money you have these days," she explained, "Is still stored in banks — but instead of paper receipts, they are recorded on your devices.

"Your phone, your computer, even your smartwatch!"

"This is where your allowance lives now."

Goldie floated backward. "In numbers. In apps. In clouds!"

A smiling cartoon dollar waved from the screen.

"No coins needed—just tap and pay!"

Noah and Midas waved back.

Suddenly, a robot zipped by, its LED eyes flashing: BITCOIN.

"Who are you- a transformer?" Noah called out.

BITCOIN
"Welcome to the digital
World of Money!"

"I'm digital gold, and I am the future," Bitcoin beeped proudly.

"No banks. Just code and math."

Noah scratched his head. "But... how do we know you are real?"

"Blockchain magic!" Bitcoin chimed, twirling like a figure skater with LED boots. "I'm encrypted- uncrackable and unstoppable!"

Noah squinted. "Okay…Money's getting super weird."

Goldie patted him on the shoulder.

"It might look wild, but it's the same old idea. *Trust* — just written in code now!"

Midas floated by and nodded.

"From fish and stone wheels, to gold coins and paper notes, money always evolved with its time."

"When our lives moved to screens, money followed. It shifted online too – invisible, but not imaginary."

Noah peered through dozens of swirling screens.

He saw a street vendor in China scan a customer's face to buy steaming dumplings, the warm mist rising around them.

Then he spotted a vending machine in Sweden that scanned a person's palm, and then it spitted out a Swedish fish candy with a cheerful wink.

Suddenly, Noah remembered the $20 bill he lost at the state fair last summer—it just vanished after the Ferris Wheel ride.

He could still recall the feeling of his stomach sinking when he reached into his pocket and it was not there.

For the rest of that day, even cotton candy tasted like regret.

"At least digital money can't fall out of my pocket,"

SWISH
"When our lives moved to screens, money followed.
It shifted online too – invisible, but not imaginary."

Noah muttered, eyeing a pixelated Bitcoin bot doing loop-de-loops overhead as people kept buying it.

Goldie nodded.

"Digital money comes with our digital life. But remember,

"What makes it work is still trust. And trust needs to be protected."

Then—

glitch.

The Bitcoin bot froze mid-air, its LED grin flickering like a birthday candle in a wind tunnel.

Noah squinted. "Uh… what happens if the Wi-Fi crashes?

Or if some genius hacker gets hangry and starts deleting people's mone*y?*"

Midas floated closer, half-joking,

"Then maybe we would all go back to using gold or bartering!"

Noah chuckled as he thought of the smelly fishes,

"Maybe we need… digital dragons to guard our treasure!"

Goldie gave a thumbs-up.

"Or at least some very good passwords!"

Just as Midas was about to say something, colorful stardust sucked Noah up like in an upside-down world.

"Wait! This isn't light—it's sugar glitter!" he yelped.

"Where's it *sticking* us now?!"

Midas' laugh crackled through the chaos.

"Maybe we are heading for a treat!"

"Wait! This isn't light—
it's sugar glitter!"

Chapter 7

Gummy Bear Economics

POP!

One moment, Noah was floating in a world of codes.

The next, his sneakers landed with a sticky squelch on the gum-splattered pavement of New York City.

He wobbled, catching his balance as car horns blared and hip-hop pounded through the humid summer air.

A flashing neon food truck loomed ahead, its sign pulsing like a carnival ride:

"Bear-y Delicious!"

"*No way*!" Noah's eyes lit up.

"That's my favorite snack!"

Before he could even pat his pockets, Midas snapped his fingers, and a crumpled dollar fluttered into Noah's hand.

Grinning, he slapped it onto the counter.

The vendor winked and handed him 4 rainbow gummy bears, their sugary scent making his mouth water.

"Sweet deal!"

Noah giggled, popping one into his mouth.

"No Way -
That's my favorite snack!"

ZAP!

The world hiccupped.

The neon billboards and food truck vanished, replaced by a drizzle-damp London street.

The scent of fresh pencil shavings and the sound of distant church bells drifted through the air.

Raindrops bounced off Noah's shoulders as he spotted another candy stand under a crooked umbrella.

A mustached man in tartan trousers bellowed:

"7 bears for a quid, lad!"

Noah's palm tingled.

His dollar transformed into a shiny British pound.

"Whoa!"

He shouted, trading it for two bags of gummies.

"More bears for the same money? Score!"

Midas nodded, floating next to him.

"It is the same amount, just in a different money —

sometimes you can get more gummy for your buck!"

Sometimes you can get
more gummy for your buck!

SWOOSH!

Without warning, the drizzle turned to a scorching desert wind, stinging Noah's cheeks with sand and the smoky scent of lamb kebabs.

In a bustling Middle Eastern souk, a street vendor was standing in front of him.

He was wearing a red-checkered shemagh, his eyes kind but serious.

"2 gummy bears for one Riyal,"

he said, holding out just two sticky treats.

Noah's mouth fell open...

then he scrunched his face.

"*Two*?! That's it?

"In London, I got way more than that!"

Midas shook his head with a chuckle.

"That's right."

"Money doesn't always stretch the same—it depends on where you are, how much of it there is, and how badly people want things."

He paused, floating a little lower.

"Over time, money also… loses strength, if you don't grow and invest it.

"Quietly. Like air leaking out of a balloon."

"Money doesn't always stretch the same."

FLASH!

The heat retreated.

Noah can see Shanghai's skyline flared around them, pulsing with holograms and occasional drones.

A robot chef in a porcelain toque politely placed a single gummy bear on a fancy white plate.

"1 yuan. 1 gummy bear," it announced.

"Optimal sweetness efficiency."

Noah groaned,

"*One*?! That's it?!"

He gave the gummy bowl a dramatic sigh, then popped the lone bear into his mouth like it was his last meal.

"Why is the price different for the exact *same* candy?"

Midas floated down beside him, chuckling.

"Because each country's money has its own kind of power," he said.

"The stronger it is, the more it can buy."

He eyed the half-melted gummy near his foot and carefully scooted away.

"Sweet when you're buying... but sour when you're selling."

"So it's like..." Noah mumbled mid-chew,

"every country speaks its own money language?"

Midas nodded. "Exactly. And the way we 'translate' between those money languages?

"1 yuan. 1 gummy bear.
Optimal sweetness efficiency."

"It's called an exchange rate—

"the math that decides how much one country's money is worth compared to another's."

Noah perked up.

"So if gummy bears are cheaper somewhere else… I can ask Mom to vacation there?"

Midas burst out laughing.

"That, little one, is the sweet science of gummy bear economics!"

Noah grinned, thinking of Mandarin lessons with his cousins in China.

Money was like a language, each with its own rules, its own power.

But before he could daydream about international gummy bear shopping sprees, a cool, damp mist began curling around his ankles.

Unlike the bright, bubbly lights from before, this mist felt grey and quiet.

It tugged at him gently, pulling him away.

He barely noticed Midas's glance—

a tiny flicker of unease and something else in Midas's golden eyes, as they slipped into time once more.

A tiny flicker of unease and something else flashed in Midas's golden eyes.

Chapter 8

The Golden Rule of Money

Silence.

Noah opened his eyes.

No clatter, no chatter, no bursting colors.

Just cool darkness and the whisper of distant echoes.

And… No Midas?

Suddenly—a *sniffle*. A quiet, shaky sob.

Noah's breath hitched. He heard it again.

A muffled cry, fragile as a penny slipping through fingers, rolling toward a storm drain.

He took off running and followed it.

He ran down vast marble halls, past the golden columns, and around the bubbling fountains that trickled streams like liquid silver.

The stillness pressed in, thick and strange.

Then, he stopped.

There, at the far end, underneath a vaulted ceiling dusted with stars, sat a king.

Tall.

Regal.

Alone on a gem-studded throne, with eyes full of sorrow.

His right hand shimmered, stiff and solid, like the weight of gold itself.

Beside him stood the most beautiful golden statue Noah had ever seen.

It was a dancing princess caught mid-twirl, arms open and face lit with joy.

So lifelike, it seemed she might spin away any second.

Silence.
Suddenly - a quiet, shaky sob.

But she didn't.

She was utterly still.

Noah stared, heart pounding. He could almost hear her laughter echoing off the walls.

Suddenly —

"Noah."

The voice was familiar, but barely a whisper.

From behind a pile of gold coins, Midas appeared. His glow was dimmer now, his smile gone. He looked at the king.

At the girl.

At the past.

"That... was *me.*"

Noah's eyes widened. He couldn't believe it.

"When I was a King," Midas began, his words slow and heavy,

"I begged the gods for gold. Endless gold."

"I thought it would make me happy. Important. *Loved.*"

His voice cracked like old parchment.

"They granted me the Golden Touch. And I went wild."

"I turned everything I touched to gold. Roses into glittering statues, bread into metal. My throne became solid sunlight."

A broken and hollow sound escaped him—

Not quite a laugh, not quite a sob.

"But then," he whispered, "I lost her."

His gaze fell to the golden princess, his voice was raw, like wind through dead leaves.

His right hand shimmered, stiff and solid,
like the weight of gold itself.

"My daughter, Zoe."

"She ran to hug me, like she always did. And I… I forgot. I reached for her."

One trembling breath.

"She turned into gold. Right in my arms."

Midas sagged, as if the weight of a thousand mountains sat on his shoulders.

Noah held his breath, his hands covering his mouth.

"I tried to fix it," he continued slowly, "I offered the gods every coin I have, every treasure I own, even my life—anything.

"But it was too late."

He reached out to brush the statue's cheek.

But his golden fingers left no warmth.

Noah's chest hurt, thinking of his mom's warm hugs, his grandma's gentle tickles, and his brother's clumsy tackles.

And to ever lose them…

He swallowed hard.

"I'm sorry," Noah said, voice shaking.

"I'm so sorry, Midas."

Midas didn't look up.

"I traded love for greed," his voice low and hollow.

"And now… I am just a coin, rolling through time, trying to warn others before it's too late."

Noah felt tears sting his eyes.

"She turned into gold.
Right in my arms."

Thinking of his mom's warm hugs,
his grandma's gentle tickles, and his
brother's clumsy tackles.

Midas turned to Noah, his glow flickering like a short candle in the wind.

"If I could, I'd trade every ounce of gold—every treasure—just for one more dance with my daughter."

Noah stepped forward without thinking.

He hugged Midas tight, the coin warm and solid against his chest.

Midas hugged him back.

His voice steadied, and he managed the tiniest smile.

"Real wealth… is the love you share, the kindness you give.

"Not the glitter you chase."

And in that hug,

Noah didn't just want to feel the **power of money.**

He wanted to understand it.

Control it.

Use it for good.

For the first time,

he wanted to have **power over money**.

Noah turned around to look at the golden princess one last time.

And for one impossible second…he saw a slight smile forming on her face.

Before Noah could look again to confirm, the wave of light spiraled around them again —

Shimmering, spiraling, lifting them high and away.

"Real wealth... is the love you share,
the kindness you give.
Not the glitter you chase."

Chapter 9

Goodbye... For Now

"This is goodbye for now, little one.”

Midas pressed gently into Noah's palm as they whirled back through time.

Noah's bedroom flickered into view—

his Star Wars comforter, the glow-in-the-dark stars, and Rexy the plush dinosaur flopped on the beanbag chair.

But for a heartbeat...

he didn't want to let go.

"Soon, we will meet again.”

Midas's voice lingered, soft and magnetic, like the last chord of a lullaby.

"Next time, we'll learn about...

"**How to Make Money!**”

Noah grinned.

"I can't wait!”

"Money opens doors...
but only people make it home."

As his eyelids drooped, the tick of Grandpa's pocket watch echoed in the quiet.

The one with no price tag, only memories.

And as sleep gently pulled Noah under,

one thought rose like a whisper to the surface:

"Money opens doors…but only people make it home."

Bonus Activities

DESIGN YOUR OWN MONEY

If you could invent your own currency, what would it look like? Draw your bill or coin below!

NAME _______________________

VALUE ____________   COUNTRY

What makes your money valuable?

Who trusts it?

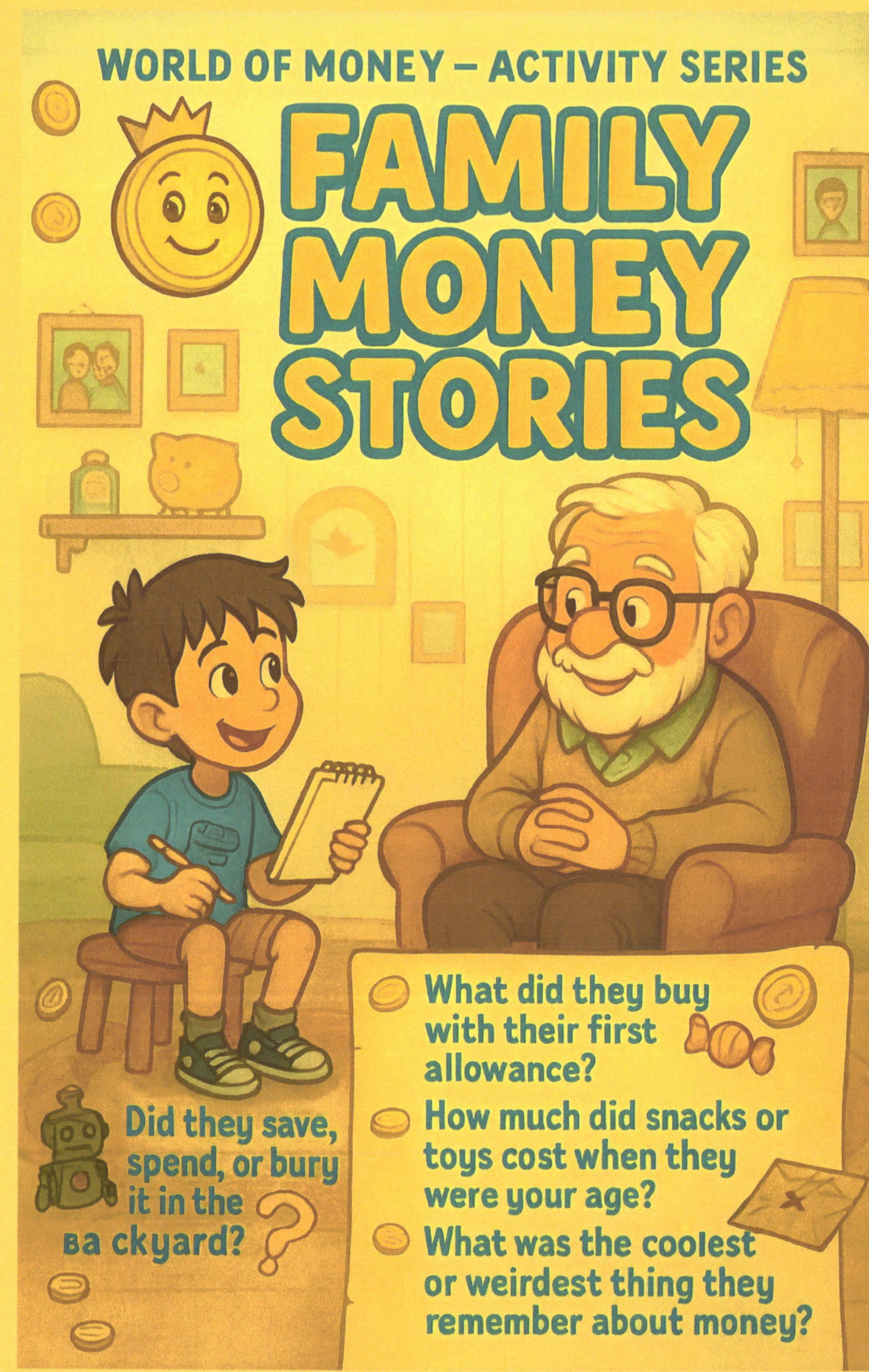

WORLD OF MONEY – ACTIVITY SERIES
FAMILY MONEY STORIES
What did they buy with their first allowance?
How much did snacks or toys cost when they were your age?
What was the coolest or weirdest thing they remember about money?
Did they save, spend, or bury it in the ва ckyard?

www.ingramcontent.com/pod-product-compliance
Lightning Source LLC
Chambersburg PA
CBHW041731300726

48981CB00005B/317